AMAZING GUIDES ON GETTING TO KNOW PEOPLE

Discovering the most effective ways of understanding the different personalities of people.

Jeffrey Brickhouse

Table of Contents

Introduction

You are undoubtedly interested in people, inquisitive about what goes through other people's thoughts, and seeking to learn more about the reasons behind people's actions if you are reading this. Determining whether anything significant is relevant may be challenging, particularly since our opinions are heavily considered. Examine individuals? Adorable. I believe that was referred to as stalking.

Joking aside, I believe you may now possess the mental agility to understand the feelings of others. Everyone has the capacity for interpersonal understanding, and our ability to do so has evolved. Understanding others to establish a connection or remain in the group was, at one point, deemed a necessary skill for survival. Natural selection might be at work here. Your scientific viewpoint on the world could also be the cause of this. Perhaps you try to observe people's facial expressions to get a sense of their thoughts and adopt a different perspective.

Chapter 1

Assessing and researching on individuals

People generally dislike being forced to do anything. Children are never asked by their parents if they want to attend school. They decide what is right in their opinion and enroll their children in the best schools and colleges because they can't possibly ask such a small child that question.

The kids feel under pressure to learn and to do well in their studies. Now that these kids are adults, the cycle keeps going. This is where the enjoyment of doing something because you enjoy it is absent. All that is being threatened is that unpleasant things will happen if you don't. Studying is motivated by fear rather than pleasure. That's not to say that some people don't love to study; in fact, some of them live for it, and they study as much as they can on their own volition without worrying about grades or other outcomes.

The importance of studying people in our situation will depend on whether we see people and their societies as something that "simply exists" or as something to think about, consider, or be fascinated by. If we think it is a waste of our limited time to research others, it may also mean that we don't think we are worthy of being studied.

That's a valid philosophical claim, but to prove it, we would need to present research topics that aren't compromised or influenced by social interactions. Denying this is rejecting the idea that our perceptions, our values, and our opinions about the topics we study are the only things that help us navigate the world. Even if we set out to study something unrelated to ourselves, we would eventually give up because nothing is more colored by the nuances of our experiences as human beings and no view from nowhere than the time, space, location, and speed of the phenomena we see and ourselves, since almost all of our mental abilities are dependent on these parameters.

To whom is it significant?

People research is important, though not as philosophical, for those who wish to understand who puts together the "dome of many-colored glass" that is society, and in what role for whom, what interests them, and why. As an alternative, individuals who are interested in "how society works," "how it stays together," "what makes it work," "what happens when things go wrong," and "the center cannot hold" may be assumed that people are drawn to other people because they are people. Those who are gregarious, curious, interested in the intricate web of social interactions, and who would rather be a part of it than be alone, accountable to no one, or private. On the other hand, people who think that people are just "vile polluted lumps of the earth" or that they can be "classified like insects" based only on traits, social status, and roles that function as a clockwork mechanism that excludes human interaction, proximity, or closeness may not think that studying people is important.

Is human behavior exclusively studied by social scientists?

However, studying people in this manner— as humans rather than as a condensed mass of organisms devoid of free will and agency that perform tasks determined by their genetic makeup—is not the only method available. Not only that, but it's unique not as a trademarked product but as a way of thinking, a "quality of mind" whose worth lies in its intellectual habit, an attitude even, that encourages us to think critically, creatively, and humorously about the world around us. It can be called by many different names and placed into a variety of categories. More significant than its name, though, is its capacity to convey information "imaginatively, and with an element of personality"—a highly esteemed mental ability. All of this goes far beyond simple proclamations in favor of one's career, despite the appearance to the contrary. Conducting personal studies with social science approaches and viewpoints is more than just a set of "useless frills."

Instead, studying people equips us with "skills that are needed to keep democracies alive," like "the ability to imagine sympathetically the predicament of another person," "the ability to think critically," and "the ability to transcend local loyalties and to approach world problems as a "citizen of the world" .

Observation

Learning about human behavior requires making observations. Understanding someone's behavior is best accomplished by watching them in action. In what manner are they interacting with a child, a patient, or a computer?

Studies based on observations

Using video is another great way to observe people. The use of video greatly expands the scope of any study project. Annotating videos allows for the creation of frame-accurate descriptions of behavior. Viso provides the video content needed to gain an understanding of processes, communication, and human performance. For recording audio and video in multiple rooms at high quality, this is the ideal choice.

Investigating the functioning of the brain

Analyzing an individual's internal anatomy, or brain, is another way to investigate their behavior. Since most of our internal processes go unnoticed, examining brain activity can offer new insights into human behavior. When studying how brain injury affects patients, for example, correlations between brain activity and behavior can be observed. There are times when brain research sheds light on enduring mysteries that psychologists have found difficult to solve.

Chapter 2

Acknowledgment as a Human Need

Recognization and acknowledgment from others are necessities for all individuals. When people ignore or forget who we are after we've met, it bothers us. The desire for acceptance forms the foundation of the human psyche. Oftentimes, it stems from a need for acceptance, acknowledgment, and a sense of significance. Incentives, successes, and social validation are just a few examples of the various ways that people can be motivated and influenced by appreciation.

In recent decades, the politics of recognition has become a central theme in political and social theories about justice and freedom. The need to be acknowledged, valued, respected, and taken into consideration by others—whether they be strangers or members of social groups—has been identified as one of the fundamental human needs. Failure to recognize others for who they are as human beings or as distinct identities deserving of respect or esteem frequently leads to a fundamentally unfair political and social climate.

Acknowledgment serves as the foundation for the allocation of all other rights, responsibilities, money, and assets. This discourse revolves around the central tenet that an individual's identity, or self-perception of who she is, her legal rights and protections, and her social and political standing in any organized community, are all shaped by the recognition or misrecognition of some other person. Some groups of people may be severely deprived of their fundamental rights as members of a political community if political societies simply deny them the right to exist as individuals.

According to Charles Taylor, people can suffer enormous psychic damage as well as actual harm when they are in social or political environments that reflect a negative self-image. Academic research has demonstrated that numerous significant cultural, ethnic, racial, gender, and religious movements of the last decade have their roots in the fight for others to recognize and value an individual's identity.

Recognition is a must for everyone. That has nothing to do with immaturity, conceit, or selfishness. From their very first moments of life, people must love and respect them. This is where we implicitly find that true acknowledgment of our humanity.

Our worth as precious, precious people is acknowledged. In addition to our accomplishments and advancements, we are recognized for our virtues. Our capacity to be moral, happy, mature adults. Our personal development and self-esteem are enhanced by the strength of those intimate relationships. The first members of society to show us love, respect, and dignity are our parents and family.

It improves our self-esteem to be respected and acknowledged. However, proceed with caution! Acknowledging people and expressing respect and belief in them is essential; acceptance is just one side of the story. The reason I regard you is because I see your potential. I am a part of your existence.

It is imperative that you expressly recognize After all, there's still something we need to be clear about even though we've been discussing the fundamental understanding that serves as the cornerstone of the concept of self-esteem. Should you not know one, you should know of someone who is constantly seeking recognition from others.

When we go beyond an unhealthy need for approval, we are in danger of becoming obsessed with having our words, deeds, behavior, attitudes, and even our physical appearance validated. To find what we cannot find within, we look outside of ourselves. Everyone needs to be acknowledged by their friends, family, and partners, but not in an intrusive or persistent way—that would be a blatant lack of confidence in myself. Subsequently, my self-assurance would diminish.

In human nature, acknowledgment is basic. We can proceed with confidence knowing it. We must also exercise it inside of ourselves to awaken it like an inner engine that can give us steadiness, confidence, and strength.

Recognization and sense of worth

Prioritizing our value, let us restate the fundamental principles that support it:

Self-honor is highly important. We won't have anything at all if you don't even think you're a valuable person with a lot of worth. Love never comes from outside sources. I can almost do anything if I accept who I am, celebrate all that I have to offer, and have the freedom to be happy.

I recognize my advantages and disadvantages. As I navigate life, I have faith in my ability to make cool, collected decisions. I feel less in control of my life when my confidence declines. Relying on someone else to handle it could make things worse.

It weakens our sense of identity when people don't even acknowledge us; we feel like we don't exist, at least not to them. The necessity for acceptance is not nearly as basic as this.

We connect with others when we are acknowledged, even for a brief moment. Bonding and the merging of identities are being achieved with this step.

Before an individual is allowed to join a group and fulfill their desire for belonging, they must first receive acknowledgment—that is, recognition of who they are—approval—and acceptance. Additional validation bestows upon them dignity, respect, and a corresponding status that grants them authority and leverage.

Neglecting people can be a tactic used for control. Individuals at the top of the tree appear to disregard those at the bottom. Their superiority is indicated by this.

Then what?

Consider the people in your immediate vicinity for a moment. Do not merely stroll by. Say hello and smile at them. It's better to look at them, even if only briefly.

Instead of taking it personally when you are ignored, you can choose to engage in thought-provoking experiments such as responding with an equal lack of attention or confronting them directly to force an acknowledgment. To 'accidentally' run into them is a straightforward move. Watch what they say or do and say nothing.

Recognizing and Expressing gratitude is essential.

Everybody needs to be acknowledged. Money isn't always the strongest thing. You could even argue that money is a kind of compensation for the labor we do. Recognition has a powerful healing effect, whether it is for us or those around us.

Recognition vs. Expression of Gratitude

Recognition and gratitude are sometimes confused. But recognition has more depth to it than that. I use compliments or praise to show someone how much I value them. I express my gratitude to someone by saying something like, "Thank you for having me here today."

Recognizing, however, entails more than simply expressing gratitude. This implies that I view them for the contributions they make to society and the world. As such, I thank them and publicly acknowledge them or their contributions.

People will feel important when I acknowledge them. "Thank you for inviting me today," is how I express my gratitude to people instead. Being with you brings me such joy. I feel motivated by you to achieve more.

This last comment demonstrates your understanding of their efforts and their influence on you.

Consequence of Recognition

I know someone will feel appreciated or loved because I appreciate their work. The reason for this is that I feel appreciated when I am acknowledged. My acknowledgment alone demonstrates my grace and social awareness.

A person's overall performance is positively impacted by being acknowledged, particularly at work. When I am appreciated for taking the initiative to complete extra work, for example, I am content. The next time, I'll perform even better as a result.
Recognizing Your Own Worth Is Essential

Acknowledging ourselves is the first step towards being able to recognize others. Acknowledging others will come more naturally when we see our worth and accomplishments.

In addition, the following reasons make acknowledging oneself crucial:

Enhances Drive

My yardstick for success is achievement. That being said, there is a drawback when I limit what counts as "achievements" to only noteworthy accomplishments. Occasionally, I become so consumed with the big picture that I overlook the little accomplishments I have made. So when I don't accomplish a major goal, I burn out.

Yet it gives me motivation when I decide to acknowledge and appreciate even modest successes. I should continue on my current path, it says. Additionally, it makes tasks seem more doable and helps me become more in line with my objectives.

Enhances Self-Belief

When I accept who I am, I feel more confident and motivated as well. It encourages me to work harder when I know that I have accomplished a goal, no matter how small. That's because I am confident in my ability to succeed.

My ability to see my abilities, commitment, and diligence comes from self-acknowledgment. I realize I can't accomplish my aim without these.

That being said, I tend to forget that I am a skilled, passionate, dedicated person when I don't acknowledge my accomplishments. As a result of my lack of self-confidence, I will eventually feel unhappy and might even experience anxiety or despair.

Techniques for Celebrating Our Triumphs

Because we don't know how we typically don't recognize our accomplishments. Luckily, I've discovered how to acknowledge my achievements in the following ways;

1. Analyze All of Your Successes, No Matter How Little

Every essential I need is on my list, and I never forget any when I head to the grocery store. To help me remember what needs to be done, I even make a list of the tasks I must accomplish.

In the same way, I discovered that it's helpful to make a list of all of my accomplishments, big and small, weekly and daily, and short- and long-term.

This allows me to see my victories along the way, which makes me feel like I'm making progress. In addition, putting them in writing helps me recall those moments, along with any difficulties I may have faced and how I resolved them.

Seeing my accomplishments to date and being reminded of my potential are both aided by keeping a list.

2. Revel in

Having a celebration is another way to recognize achievement. Although it is not required, you are welcome to throw a lavish celebration. For example, I don't need much to treat myself to a quick hike.

The important thing is to reward yourself with something joyful after you achieve something. Suppose you've finished the laundry that had been neglected for several weeks. Give yourself a wonderful meal as a way to celebrate. Acknowledging our accomplishments through small victories is not a self-centered or egotistical gesture.

The "Jar of Cookies"

I have encountered numerous ups and downs in my pursuit of my objectives. I've occasionally found myself in the fetal position sobbing because the difficulties have occasionally been so difficult to handle. However, before reaping numerous successes, David Goggins faced great adversity. This was the "Cookie Jar," as he put it.

He uses his cookie jar as a metaphor for remembering accomplishments during difficult times. It also helps me access my sympathetic nervous system, which is another reason I practice this. Thus, even when things seem too difficult, I can find the motivation to press on.

By keeping in mind what it's like to be successful when I achieve my goals, I adhere to the cookie jar theory. Consequently, it will aid in my memory of how life challenged me and how I overcame such obstacles.

Remind yourself that you are capable of more by thinking back on your successes and mentally reliving the occasion.

Chapter 3

Understanding a Person's Life Situation

Although humans are capable of gaining knowledge from the experiences of others, we frequently refuse to do so. Maybe this is because we believe that we would never experience something similar. Maybe this is because we think that, in the same circumstances, we would choose differently.

We might assume that objective data gathered from the outside world is more reliable than an individual's subjective experience, which could be the reason. Academics must draw lessons from the experiences of others, regardless of the presumptions that underlie this concern. Indeed, it is a fundamental tenet of research. To gather data or develop a fresh understanding of a subject, researchers carefully examine individuals, groups of individuals, societies, or objects. To gain fresh perspectives on a given phenomenon, conducting such in-depth research frequently necessitates comprehending the experiences of others.

The worlds we live in today and our ancestors' are very different. The problems of today, many of which are man-made, can be understood and solutions found, though, if we first understand who we are and how the past has shaped us. Understanding what characteristics of human nature are constant and what we can and should actively change will help us secure the future for both our world and ourselves.

The story of the human journey is the mind's evolution, the world it built, the problems it solved, the rationale behind those solutions, how those solutions shaped the mind's subsequent decisions, and so on.

Things that we used to think were unique to the human brain are derived from other animals, according to recent research. Rats are willing to give up food for one another, even if they are strangers. Many animals, like bonobos, show empathy, generosity, and a sense of fairness. Despite the widespread belief that morality developed in religion, morality is now understood to be an innate trait shared by humans and other animals. Though they were often misunderstood, all of our prophets and spiritual leaders mentioned this: a more complete understanding can stabilize in the brain through the cultivation of a necessary "selflessness," which is made possible by virtues that were once widely believed to provide "a ticket to heaven." Scientists studying neurobiology and evolution psychology now concur.

The brain is pliable in humans. It has allowed us to adapt, survive, and even flourish wherever we are in the world. Only humans are capable of doing this. One of the disadvantages of our flexibility is that we are easily influenced and swayed by the group or culture we belong to. Even though our minds are trained to see the world in terms of "Us and Them," humans are social animals by nature and are designed to interact with people outside of our immediate social group. Scholars, intellectuals, and psychologists have once more highlighted this. The scholar Idries Shah most succinctly perhaps most recently did so in the book Reflections:

Tolerance and an attempt to comprehend others, which were once regarded as luxury items, are now necessary. This is because, if we fail to see that our behavior and that of others is primarily the result of deeply rooted prejudices that we are ignorant of and confuse for our own beliefs, we might act in ways that will ultimately result in the extinction of humanity. By then, it will be too late to determine whether tolerance is a positive or negative trait.

People can't handle prejudice because they're trying to treat the symptoms. Bias is the symptom; incorrect assumptions are the cause. "Assumption gives birth to prejudice." The advancements in science and technology, including research on animal and primate behavior, psychology, and neuroscience, have allowed us to reconsider what it means to be human.

The most important inheritance that humans have received is the capacity to transcend our inheritance. This has been our constant course of action. We can trace our ancestry back to Africa, our spread across the globe, and the various groups, tribes, city-states, and civilizations we have given rise to throughout history. We can examine the history and rationale behind the establishment of our political, religious, economic, ecological, educational, and humanitarian institutions.

The world we live in today and our ancestors' are very different. Understanding who we are and how history has shaped us will help us better understand and address today's issues, many of which are man-made. To aid in our evolution, we need to know which facets of human nature are constant and which ones we can and ought to actively change. It will help us to move forward to realize that human history began over 300,000 years ago. one that only belongs to people.

The formation of human behaviors

To create strong emotional bonds, organizations must comprehend why people feel and act the way they do in addition to acknowledging and managing the relationship between experiences, emotions, and actions.

However, given how complex people are, this can be challenging. We don't make perfectly logical decisions based only on devoid of emotion or sentiment. Numerous other unseen factors also affect our behavior. Organizations will struggle to consistently deliver engaging experiences if they do not recognize and address these underlying determinants, which are frequently unconscious. Thankfully, there are certain essential traits that everyone possesses. Organizations will be able to establish strong and enduring relationships if they acknowledge and value the Six Essential Characteristics of People;

Intuition: Individuals make decisions in two distinct ways: quickly, instinctively, and predicated on biases and mental shortcuts, and slowly, logically, and deliberately. People mostly use the latter approach, referred to as "Intuitive Thinking," when making decisions, particularly in stressful or emergencies. Regretfully, rather than satisfying our intuitive side, most organizations spend excessive amounts of time attempting to appeal to our rational side.

Selfishness: Everybody has a distinct and personal perspective on the world. This reality makes it challenging to imagine ourselves in other people's situations. Understanding this natural egotism will enable you to see and address the problems that arise.

Emotional: Individuals tend to recall events according to their emotional state, especially at the highest and lowest points of an encounter – a phenomenon called the Peak-End Rule. Consider in advance the emotions you want the experience to evoke at these crucial moments as you design it.

Motivated: A sense of competence, control, advancement, and purpose are the four basic human needs that people work to satisfy. Instead of concentrating only on extrinsic needs like price and monetary compensation, make sure you're designing customer and employee experiences that meet these intrinsic needs.

Social: People are drawn to those who are "like them," and they tend to trust these individuals or organizations more than others. Acknowledge the significant influence that people's social groups have over one another, and look for opportunities to assist staff members and clients in developing deep relationships. Go here to read more about experience design that is infused with emotion.

Optimistic: People react favorably to optimism and hope, and they thrive on it. Successful companies inspire the individuals within their ecosystem by presenting a vision of future achievement that takes into account each person's unique needs and goals.

Why is human behavior significant?

Client, workers, associates, Providers. What has each of these groups in common? They are all composed of individuals. All individuals who come into contact with your organization are unique, and their perceptions and emotions regarding their interactions with your company will influence their allegiance to it and, eventually, your financial performance.

But before you can manage experiences effectively, you need to know what people in your ecosystem need and want. To do this, one must first accept and accommodate people's actual thoughts and feelings before converting those insights into interesting experiences. With our free design worksheet, you can look for chances to create more engaging experiences.

Recognizing the fundamentals of human behavior

Humans interact with the outside world through their experiences. They can be as enlightening as answering a work email or as transformative as becoming a parent.

This implies that every time a person engages with a company, they will have an experience. And that encounter, be it ordinary, revolutionary, or somewhere in between, will elicit an emotional reaction from them that will shape their views and guide their conduct going forward. such as whether they make more purchases, tell friends about the company, or stay late at work.

Organizations must thus understand how people's experiences influence their thoughts, feelings, and behaviors toward their brand to influence profitable behaviors. But it's not enough to just acknowledge this connection. Organizations must actively manage the five components of the human experience cycle to influence how individuals interpret and react to their experiences;

Experiences: The real-life events that transpire in a person's course of interactions.

Expectations: What a person believes will occur during a particular experience.

Perceptions: The way a person interprets an experience based on their expectations, which are measured in terms of effort (how easy or difficult it was), emotion (how they felt), and success (whether they were able to accomplish their goal).

Attitudes: The beliefs and feelings a person has about the company. The way a person behaves in an organization is largely determined by their attitudes.

Gains have less of an impact on people than losses do. Unconsciously weighing the possible benefits and drawbacks of each option, we make decisions rather than considering the outcome rationally. Simplicity is preferred over complexity by people. Even in situations where a more complex option would be preferable, people often go for the one that is easiest for them to mentally process. We prefer plain language over corporate jargon and perplexing buzzwords, and the same holds for communications.

People are impacted by those in our immediate vicinity. That brings us full circle to one of the six essential characteristics of humans: our social nature. Consequently, people frequently submit to the wisdom of the masses (also known as "jumping on the bandwagon") or to those whom we regard as "experts."

The visceral and emotional states that people are in influence their behavior. People's behaviors are influenced by their emotions during an experience. People act more impulsively, for instance, when they are hungry. They use Intuitive Thinking more when they are feeling strong emotions. By keeping this in mind, you can take measures to calm down irate clients before approaching them with a reasonable proposition, like a fix for their problem.

Context influences people's decision-making. Not all decisions are made in a vacuum; context plays a crucial role in helping people make decisions. Examples of context include the physical setting in which they make decisions, the effects of unconscious priming, the framing of a decision, and the alternatives they can compare it to.

Many misinterpret what we have experienced in the past and what lies ahead. We use our memories to judge our experiences in retrospect rather than viewing them as a continuous loop of video in our minds. Additionally, we have trouble predicting the future or ourselves with any degree of accuracy. Instead of treating people like perfectly logical, rational beings, organizations that can create experiences that mirror how people think and behave will be able to connect emotionally with their audience, which will ultimately lead to greater loyalty and increased revenue.

Chapter 4

Handling people's diverse personalities

The distinctive patterns of emotions, ideas, and actions that set an individual apart from others are referred to as their personality. It is a lifelong trait that is largely determined by biology and environment. The characteristics we describe about other people are examples of personality. Take statements like "They are loyal and protective of their friends" or "She is generous, caring, and a bit of a perfectionist," as examples of a person's personality can be explained by a multitude of factors, from hereditary impacts to the influence of personal experiences and surroundings. One of the first things we notice about the people around us is how different from one another they are. While some people are very quiet, others are very talkative. While some people like to lounge around, others are active. Some seem anxious rarely, while others worry a great deal. When we describe people around us with adjectives like "talkative," "quiet," "active," or "anxious," we are referring to their personalities—the distinctive qualities that set them apart from one another.

Does a stable personality mean that personality changes nothing? You most likely recall how your personal experiences—such as your upbringing and the care you received—have shaped who you are today. You may also recall the highs and lows you've had throughout your life. Personality can indeed change over extended periods. As we age, our openness to new experiences tends to wane, but between the ages of 20 and 40, we tend to become more emotionally stable, more conscientious (organized and dependable), and more socially dominant. Put another way, change happens to personalities even though we consider them to be generally stable. Furthermore, our personalities are important and have an impact on us even as young children. Research demonstrates, for instance, that our early personalities may account for a portion of our later career success and job satisfaction.

Qualities of the Personality

What precisely comprises a personality type? These core aspects of personality, along with traits and thought and emotion patterns, are significant:

Regularity: Behaviors typically exhibit a discernible regularity and order. In essence, individuals behave similarly or identically in a range of circumstances.

Psychological as well as physical: Although research indicates that biological processes and needs also have an impact on personality, personality is primarily a psychological construct. It impacts our actions and behaviors In addition to affecting our actions and reactions in our surroundings, personality also drives our behavior.

Several ways to say it: Beyond behavior, personality is shown in other ways as well. It also shows up in our emotions, thoughts, intimate relationships, and other social interactions.

Types of Personality

According to type theories, the number of personality types that can be linked to biological factors is restricted. According to one theory, there are four different personality types. These are:

Type A: They are aggressive, workaholic, impatient,competitive, achievement-oriented, perfectionist, and stressed

Type B: They are easygoing, patient, creative, flexible, and change-adaptive; has a propensity to put things off.

Type C: They are Extremely meticulous, perfectionistic, and unable to express both positive and negative emotions

Type D: They usually seem bleak and hopeless, worries a lot, gets angry easily, is irritable, pessimistic, avoids social situations, lacks confidence, and fears being rejected.

Personality Characteristics includes;

Concurrency: Considers others, possesses empathy, and takes pleasure in lending a hand to others.

Eager to please: Compliant, submissive, and willing to comply.

Extraversion: Exuberance, friendliness, talkativeness, assertiveness, and a high degree of emotional expressiveness are characteristics of extraversion.

Neuroticism: Feels anxious, worries about various things, becomes angry easily, experiences stress and abrupt mood swings, and finds it difficult to recover from stressful situations.

Openness: Highly imaginative, willing to attempt new things, and focused on taking on novel challenges.

From research and studies, some strategies worked well for handling people's differences within an organization and they expansiated below:

1. Practice self-kindness;
Self-respect is the prerequisite for self-awareness. Respect for others stems from understanding and valuing your identity, perspective, and abilities. When there is a solid basis of mutual respect, disagreements can be settled peacefully.

2. Make common goals the top priority;

When attempting to manage different personalities at work, your team's shared goals serve as the greatest unifier. The notion of "team players" originates from the shared sense of belonging to the same team. Colleagues who are more assertive or dominant than you don't have to be your subordinates; you don't have to back down or silence yourself to work as a team. To work with diverse personalities, all you need to do is make your ultimate goal your priority.

3. Steer clear of making arguments personal;
When working with people who have different personalities, disagreements can feel personal. It's acceptable to feel offended

when someone disregards your opinions or treats you with disrespect. However, don't interpret anything about them as personal. Their issues are what cause them to behave the way they do, not your personality. You have to learn to maintain some distance between your behavior and other people's to be a successful team manager.

4. Respect other people's contributions;
When you collaborate with individuals who possess distinct personalities, it is easy to identify the difficulties that may arise. It is less obvious how your differences can improve teamwork. To promote unity among coworkers, you have to actively seek out their positive attributes. Remember that a colleague's openness promotes effective

communication, even if you think they are being aggressive. Consider that a coworker may be trying to demonstrate empathy if you see that they are acting very passive.

5. Don't be afraid to confront arguments head-on;

Learning how to lead a diverse team requires embracing interpersonal conflict. If a dispute comes up, don't be scared to address it directly. Taking care of the issue right now will save it from getting worse, even though it may feel awkward at first. Effective conflict resolution in the workplace sets a person apart as a kind and capable leader.

Chapter 5

Building the strongest possible rapport with other people

Even though verbal communication is crucial in a business context, nonverbal cues like poise, body language, and the rapport between a company and its customers are also significant. For example, to secure future repeat business, a salesperson needs to build a productive working relationship and have a professional, goal-oriented conversation with their client. A positive, harmonious, and meaningful relationship or connection where there is mutual trust between all involved parties is known as rapport, and it is this that facilitates and strengthens business relationships. The concept of rapport can also be used to characterize each party's understanding and support for the interests of the other members of the relationship.

The act of generating a meaningful and trustworthy relationship with two or more individuals is known as rapport building. Long-term professional relationships and rapport-building can happen inadvertently when people share similar interests or behaviors, or consciously when they find things in common with each other. Because they are making enduring impressions with other professionals in a similar field, rapport enables an individual to advance their career and their capacity to effectively network with others. Since the purpose of rapport building is to highlight each party's interests, a relationship can only start to take shape after trust has been established.

How to Establish Credibility

Since establishing a rapport with someone requires an emotional connection, it is necessary to incorporate both external and personal interests in addition to common experiences, opinions, and a sense of humor. Each partner in the relationship should concentrate on balancing the needs of everyone rather than just their own or others' needs. Establishing rapport is a complex but rewarding process that calls for the commitment of all parties involved. People who prioritize their needs over others' needs, for instance, could come across as desperate or unreliable, while someone who only considers their interests might be seen as selfish by others. For a relationship to be successful and last over time, each partner must strike a balance between their own needs and those of their business partners.

The term "zone of rapport" often refers to the shared interests of two or more parties. Developing a rapport with clients is crucial because it enables effective trust-building and empathy among all parties involved. For a strong relationship to endure, all of its participants must stay in their rapport-rich area. People with the ability to quickly establish rapport and discover points of agreement with others can build the trust necessary for a business relationship to succeed. As new interests and points of commonality are found, a relationship can continue to be enjoyed while it is in the zone of rapport.

Which techniques can you use to build rapport?

Building rapport between two or more people happens through a variety of activities and exchanges. To establish a long-lasting relationship, some forms of interaction and the identification of shared interests can arise organically through frequent conversation, while others can be actively or purposely sought out.

Here are a few general strategies for establishing rapport in a professional or organizational setting:

- Make a good impression at first and ensure that everyone is at ease when interacting.

- Listen intently and focus entirely on the person speaking.

- If something is unclear, clarify it by asking questions.

- Be mindful of body language and nonverbal cues like posture, eye contact, and facial expressions.

- Try to understand other people, show empathy for them, and try to establish a personal connection by talking about a shared interest or pastime.

- Talk about and cooperatively work toward shared interests and objectives.

- Pay attention to what others have accomplished and congratulate them on it.

- Be amiable, and sincere, and resist the urge to change who you are to attract attention from others.

- Avoid passing judgment on the beliefs, perspectives, pursuits, or concepts of others.

An individual's capacity to connect with others is significantly influenced by the traits of good rapport. Building strong relationships and providing excellent customer service across various industries requires rapport in business. For a cohesive work environment to flourish, company executives must also build rapport and a trusting environment with employees.

A company's ability to maintain its reputation in the event of a mistake is facilitated by rapport, which also fosters mutual understanding between various parties. A company that has developed a strong rapport with its clients is not impervious to a disparity in the caliber of services provided; nonetheless, if a client has firmly established trust, the likelihood of the client giving the company another chance is increased. A client would not be likely to give the business another chance and might decide to do business with a rival if the company did not value building and maintaining honest and strong relationships with its clients, or if there was no opportunity for rapport to be established.

Because trust cannot be established in a relationship without rapport, it is unlikely that a person will forge a solid, enduring connection with others. As a result, one party could believe that the other party is not thinking about their best interests. In the business world, a lack of good rapport can also negatively impact the relationship between management and employees. This can lead to internal conflict, undermine a person's leadership, create mistrust in the workplace, and generally result in disgruntled employees or decreased sales. The impact of rapport on interpersonal and professional relationships and communications highlights the necessity and significance of establishing trust at the outset in a variety of contexts. Other efficient approaches to starting a conversation with someone are as follows:

1. Have direct and truthful communication
Good communication, whether it be via emails, phone calls, or in-person interactions, is crucial for thriving relationships. Being direct, honest, and professional is necessary for developing rapport and trust.

Speaking is not as important as hearing. Learning how to listen intently is helpful and builds confidence. Consider carefully before responding, and pay attention to what others are saying.

2. Develop your people skills
Your interpersonal skills are being discussed here. Your ability to build successful relationships will be enhanced by

developing your people skills. Consider your approach to conflict and your awareness of your advantages and disadvantages. The ability to recognize how your emotions affect you and those around you is known as emotional intelligence and it is something you can work on improving.

3. Respect and cherish other individuals
Rewarding others is a great way to deepen your relationship with them. Don't focus just on winning over upper management; instead, make time for everyone, regardless of their position. If you commit to a task, see that it is completed. Try your best to always meet deadlines and requests. Simply put, treat people how you want to be treated.

4. Accept it and give it as a sign of support.
Offering your expertise, knowledge, and time shows others how valuable you are and can lead to successful partnerships. Therefore, be proactive, help others, and grasp every opportunity to provide support. In addition to sharing your knowledge, don't be ashamed to ask for help or advice. Make use of the skills and knowledge that people have; most people are happy to assist and like feeling helpful.

5. Keep a positive outlook
It's easy to get sucked into office politics and gossip in an attempt to fit in, but try not to give in to the temptation. Keep your composure and approach any issues with a positive attitude.

When there is mutual trust and understanding amongst all parties involved, a positive and meaningful relationship or connection is formed, known as rapport. To build a healthy working relationship, each partner in the relationship acknowledges both their own needs and interests as well as those of the other partners. Not only does rapport establish a solid, enduring connection between the two people, but it also influences a person's capacity for constructive or forward-thinking social interaction.

Conclusion

Fundamentally, learning about others enables you to comprehend how they think and is a key component of getting to know them. When you are interacting with friends, family, coworkers, employers, and clients, this knowledge is very helpful. When you grasp the key ideas needed to create harmonious relationships with those around you, developing strong interpersonal relationships becomes easier.

You can learn about people's thoughts, emotions, and behaviors by studying them. Your people skills will improve if you have a deeper comprehension of the intentions and motivations underlying human behavior. This will assist you in handling situations in life where you can apply your knowledge to defuse tense situations and create enduring relationships.

Studying people in their private lives has numerous other advantages. You have improved self-perception in addition to developing a deeper understanding of other people. Because of this, psychology is a great self-help tool that can assist you in overcoming phobias, stress, and anxiety.

You will be able to address the root cause of your negative thought patterns and change your negative thought patterns by studying people.

www.ingramcontent.com/pod-product-compliance
Lightning Source LLC
Chambersburg PA
CBHW061004260726
48661CB00005B/2041